EMMANUEL JOSEPH

Tech Savvy and Land Legacy, Business Tactics of Industry Giants

Copyright © 2025 by Emmanuel Joseph

All rights reserved. No part of this publication may be reproduced, stored or transmitted in any form or by any means, electronic, mechanical, photocopying, recording, scanning, or otherwise without written permission from the publisher. It is illegal to copy this book, post it to a website, or distribute it by any other means without permission.

First edition

*This book was professionally typeset on Reedsy.
Find out more at reedsy.com*

Contents

1. Chapter 1: The Digital Frontier: Embracing Technological... — 1
2. Chapter 2: Land of Opportunity: Strategic Real Estate... — 3
3. Chapter 3: Data-Driven Decisions: Harnessing the Power of... — 5
4. Chapter 4: Building Brand Reputation: The Power of Trust and... — 7
5. Chapter 5: Strategic Alliances: The Power of Collaboration — 9
6. Chapter 6: Global Expansion: Conquering New Markets — 11
7. Chapter 7: Innovation and R&D: Fueling the Future — 13
8. Chapter 8: Corporate Culture: The Heart of Innovation and... — 15
9. Chapter 9: Adaptability and Resilience: Navigating... — 17
10. Chapter 10: Corporate Social Responsibility: Making a... — 19
11. Chapter 11: Leadership: Guiding Vision and Inspiring Success — 21
12. Chapter 12: The Future: Trends and Opportunities Shaping the... — 23

1

Chapter 1: The Digital Frontier: Embracing Technological Innovation

The dawn of the digital age has brought about a seismic shift in how businesses operate. Industry giants have recognized the critical importance of embracing technological innovation to stay ahead of the competition. From automation and artificial intelligence to data analytics and blockchain, technology has become the backbone of modern business operations.

In the early 2000s, companies like Amazon and Google revolutionized the e-commerce and search engine markets by leveraging cutting-edge technologies. Amazon's implementation of sophisticated algorithms and automation streamlined their supply chain and improved customer experience. Google's pioneering search algorithms transformed how we access and process information, cementing their dominance in the tech industry.

As technology continues to advance, companies must remain agile and adaptive. Industry giants invest heavily in research and development to stay at the forefront of innovation. Apple, for example, consistently pushes the boundaries of design and functionality with each new product release, maintaining its position as a market leader.

However, technological innovation is not without its challenges. Businesses must navigate issues such as cybersecurity threats, ethical considerations, and the rapid pace of change. Industry giants that successfully overcome these obstacles are those that foster a culture of continuous learning and experimentation.

In the following chapters, we will explore how various industry leaders have harnessed the power of technology and land to build and sustain their empires. From real estate conglomerates to tech behemoths, these companies have demonstrated that the fusion of tech-savviness and strategic land acquisitions is a recipe for long-term success.

2

Chapter 2: Land of Opportunity: Strategic Real Estate Investments

While technological innovation propels businesses forward, strategic land acquisitions provide a solid foundation for long-term success. Real estate has always been a valuable asset, and industry giants have capitalized on this by securing prime locations and developing properties that enhance their operational capabilities and market presence.

One prime example is Walmart, which has meticulously chosen locations for its stores to maximize accessibility and convenience for customers. By strategically placing stores in high-traffic areas and expanding into rural communities, Walmart has built a vast network of retail outlets that contribute significantly to its market dominance. The company's real estate strategy is complemented by its advanced logistics infrastructure, ensuring efficient supply chain management.

Similarly, tech companies like Google and Apple have invested heavily in their campus environments, creating sprawling headquarters that foster innovation and collaboration. The design and location of these campuses are carefully planned to attract top talent and promote a culture of creativity. Google's Googleplex in Mountain View and Apple's Apple Park in Cupertino are iconic examples of how strategic land investments can drive business success.

In addition to commercial real estate, industry giants also recognize the value of industrial and logistics properties. Amazon's investment in fulfillment centers worldwide has revolutionized e-commerce by enabling faster delivery times and increased inventory capacity. These strategically located facilities allow Amazon to meet the demands of its global customer base efficiently.

Furthermore, the acquisition of land for renewable energy projects is becoming increasingly important. Companies like Tesla are investing in large tracts of land for solar farms and battery storage facilities, aligning with their commitment to sustainable energy solutions. These investments not only reduce operational costs but also enhance the company's brand reputation as a leader in green technology.

Strategic real estate investments provide industry giants with a competitive edge by enhancing their operational efficiency, market presence, and brand reputation. In the next chapter, we will explore how companies leverage data analytics to drive decision-making and optimize their business strategies.

3

Chapter 3: Data-Driven Decisions: Harnessing the Power of Analytics

Data has become the lifeblood of modern business, and industry giants have mastered the art of harnessing data analytics to drive decision-making and optimize their operations. By collecting, analyzing, and interpreting vast amounts of data, these companies gain valuable insights that inform their strategies and actions.

One of the pioneers in data analytics is Amazon. The company utilizes advanced data analytics to understand customer behavior, personalize recommendations, and optimize inventory management. By analyzing purchase patterns, browsing history, and customer reviews, Amazon can predict trends, tailor marketing campaigns, and ensure that products are readily available to meet customer demand.

Similarly, Netflix has revolutionized the entertainment industry by leveraging data analytics to curate personalized content for its subscribers. The company's sophisticated algorithms analyze viewing habits, preferences, and engagement metrics to recommend shows and movies that align with individual tastes. This data-driven approach has contributed significantly to Netflix's subscriber growth and retention.

In the financial sector, companies like JPMorgan Chase use data analytics to manage risk, detect fraud, and enhance customer experiences. By analyzing transaction data, the bank can identify suspicious activities, develop targeted financial products, and provide personalized financial advice to clients. Data analytics also enables the bank to optimize its operations, improve efficiency, and reduce costs.

The healthcare industry has also benefited from data analytics, with companies like IBM Watson Health using AI and machine learning to analyze medical data and improve patient outcomes. By processing vast amounts of medical records, genomic data, and clinical trial results, IBM Watson Health can identify patterns, recommend treatment options, and support medical research.

In the next chapter, we will explore how industry giants leverage their brand reputation to build customer loyalty and drive business growth. Brand reputation is a critical asset that can influence customer perceptions, attract top talent, and create lasting relationships with stakeholders.

4

Chapter 4: Building Brand Reputation: The Power of Trust and Loyalty

A strong brand reputation is a cornerstone of business success, and industry giants understand the importance of building trust and loyalty among their customers. A positive brand image can influence consumer decisions, attract top talent, and create a competitive advantage in the market.

Apple is a prime example of a company that has successfully built a strong brand reputation. The company's commitment to innovation, design excellence, and customer experience has earned it a loyal customer base. Apple's brand is synonymous with quality and reliability, and its iconic products, such as the iPhone and MacBook, are highly regarded by consumers worldwide. The company's consistent delivery of cutting-edge technology and exceptional service has solidified its position as a market leader.

Similarly, Tesla has built a strong brand reputation by positioning itself as a pioneer in electric vehicles and sustainable energy solutions. The company's commitment to innovation, environmental sustainability, and high-performance products has garnered a dedicated following of customers and investors. Tesla's brand image is further enhanced by its charismatic CEO, Elon Musk, who is known for his visionary leadership and bold ambitions.

In the retail sector, companies like Costco have earned customer loyalty through their commitment to value and quality. Costco's membership-based model, competitive pricing, and focus on customer satisfaction have created a loyal customer base that continues to drive the company's growth. The company's reputation for providing high-quality products at affordable prices has made it a trusted retailer among consumers.

Brand reputation is not just about consumer perception; it also plays a crucial role in attracting and retaining top talent. Companies with strong brand reputations are often seen as desirable employers, attracting skilled professionals who are passionate about the company's mission and values. This, in turn, contributes to the company's overall success and growth.

In the next chapter, we will delve into the importance of strategic partnerships and collaborations in driving business success. Industry giants often form alliances with other companies to enhance their capabilities, expand their reach, and create new opportunities for growth.

5

Chapter 5: Strategic Alliances: The Power of Collaboration

In an interconnected world, strategic partnerships and collaborations have become vital components of business success. Industry giants recognize the value of forming alliances with other companies to enhance their capabilities, expand their reach, and create new opportunities for growth.

A notable example is the partnership between Microsoft and LinkedIn. In 2016, Microsoft acquired LinkedIn, the world's largest professional networking platform, to integrate its services with Microsoft's productivity tools. This strategic alliance allowed Microsoft to enhance its offerings in the business and professional sectors, providing users with a seamless experience that combines social networking with productivity. The collaboration has led to the development of innovative solutions, such as LinkedIn Learning, which offers online courses and professional development resources.

Another successful collaboration is the partnership between Starbucks and Nestlé. In 2018, Starbucks and Nestlé entered into a global coffee alliance, granting Nestlé the rights to sell Starbucks-branded products outside of Starbucks stores. This partnership allowed Starbucks to expand its reach into new markets and capitalize on Nestlé's extensive distribution network. For Nestlé, the alliance provided access to Starbucks' premium coffee products, enhancing its portfolio and strengthening its position in the global coffee market.

In the automotive industry, the collaboration between Toyota and Tesla stands out. In 2010, Toyota and Tesla formed a partnership to develop electric vehicles. This alliance allowed Toyota to leverage Tesla's expertise in electric vehicle technology, while Tesla benefited from Toyota's extensive manufacturing experience. The collaboration resulted in the production of the Toyota RAV4 EV, showcasing the potential of combining the strengths of two industry leaders.

Strategic alliances also play a crucial role in the technology sector. For instance, the partnership between Apple and IBM has transformed the enterprise mobility market. In 2014, Apple and IBM joined forces to develop enterprise-grade mobile applications and solutions, combining Apple's user-friendly devices with IBM's robust analytics and enterprise software. This collaboration has empowered businesses to improve productivity, enhance customer experiences, and drive innovation through mobile technology.

Strategic partnerships and collaborations enable industry giants to leverage complementary strengths, access new markets, and drive innovation. In the next chapter, we will explore how companies navigate the complexities of global expansion and adapt to different markets to achieve sustained growth.

6

Chapter 6: Global Expansion: Conquering New Markets

Expanding into international markets is a critical growth strategy for industry giants seeking to diversify their revenue streams and achieve sustained growth. However, navigating the complexities of global expansion requires careful planning, cultural sensitivity, and adaptability.

One of the key considerations for successful global expansion is understanding and adapting to local market conditions. Industry giants must conduct thorough market research to identify consumer preferences, cultural nuances, and regulatory requirements. For example, McDonald's has successfully expanded its presence worldwide by adapting its menu to suit local tastes and preferences. In India, McDonald's offers a range of vegetarian options, including the McAloo Tikki burger, to cater to the predominantly vegetarian population.

In addition to market adaptation, industry giants must also develop robust supply chain networks to support their global operations. Companies like Amazon have invested heavily in building a global logistics infrastructure, including fulfillment centers, distribution hubs, and transportation networks. This investment enables Amazon to provide fast and reliable delivery services to customers in various regions, enhancing customer satisfaction and driving growth.

Another important aspect of global expansion is building strong relationships with local partners and stakeholders. Industry giants often form joint ventures or strategic alliances with local companies to navigate regulatory complexities and gain market insights. For instance, Starbucks entered the Chinese market through a joint venture with a local partner, maximizing its chances of success by leveraging the partner's knowledge of the market and consumer behavior.

Companies must also consider the impact of global expansion on their brand reputation and corporate social responsibility. Industry giants are increasingly aware of the importance of ethical business practices and environmental sustainability in their global operations. For example, Unilever has implemented sustainable sourcing practices and initiatives to reduce its environmental footprint, enhancing its brand reputation and building trust with consumers worldwide.

In the next chapter, we will delve into the role of innovation and research and development (R&D) in driving business growth and maintaining a competitive edge. Industry giants invest heavily in R&D to develop cutting-edge products and solutions that meet evolving consumer needs and stay ahead of the competition.

7

Chapter 7: Innovation and R&D: Fueling the Future

In a fast-paced business environment, innovation and research and development (R&D) are essential for sustaining growth and staying ahead of the competition. Industry giants invest heavily in R&D to develop cutting-edge products and solutions that meet evolving consumer needs and push the boundaries of what is possible.

One company that epitomizes the importance of R&D is Tesla. Under the leadership of Elon Musk, Tesla has revolutionized the automotive industry with its electric vehicles, autonomous driving technology, and energy storage solutions. Tesla's commitment to innovation is evident in its continuous development of advanced battery technologies, which are crucial for extending the range and performance of electric vehicles. The company's focus on R&D has not only positioned it as a leader in the electric vehicle market but also propelled advancements in renewable energy and sustainable transportation.

In the pharmaceutical industry, companies like Pfizer and Moderna have demonstrated the critical role of R&D in addressing global health challenges. The rapid development of COVID-19 vaccines was made possible by years of research and investment in mRNA technology. These companies' ability to innovate and adapt their R&D efforts in response to a global crisis highlights the importance of being prepared to tackle emerging health threats and improve public health outcomes.

Similarly, in the tech industry, companies like Alphabet (Google's parent company) invest significantly in R&D to explore new technologies and business opportunities. Alphabet's research initiatives include projects in artificial intelligence, quantum computing, and autonomous vehicles. Google's DeepMind, for instance, has made groundbreaking advancements in AI, including the development of AlphaGo, which defeated the world champion in the complex game of Go. These innovations have far-reaching implications for various industries and demonstrate the transformative potential of R&D.

Moreover, R&D is not limited to large corporations; startups and smaller companies also play a crucial role in driving innovation. Industry giants often collaborate with or acquire startups to access new technologies and tap into fresh ideas. For example, Facebook (now Meta) acquired Oculus VR, a startup specializing in virtual reality technology, to expand its presence in the emerging VR market.

In the next chapter, we will explore the role of corporate culture in driving business success. A strong and positive corporate culture can foster innovation, attract top talent, and create a cohesive and motivated workforce.

8

Chapter 8: Corporate Culture: The Heart of Innovation and Success

Corporate culture is the foundation of a company's identity and plays a pivotal role in driving business success. A strong and positive corporate culture fosters innovation, attracts top talent, and creates a cohesive and motivated workforce that is aligned with the company's mission and values.

One of the most well-known examples of a strong corporate culture is Google. Google's culture is characterized by its emphasis on creativity, collaboration, and employee well-being. The company's open and inclusive work environment encourages employees to share ideas, take risks, and think outside the box. Google's perks and benefits, such as free meals, on-site fitness centers, and flexible work hours, contribute to a positive work-life balance and employee satisfaction. This supportive culture has been instrumental in driving Google's innovation and success.

Another example is Zappos, an online shoe and clothing retailer known for its unique and customer-centric corporate culture. Zappos places a strong emphasis on delivering exceptional customer service and fostering a fun and engaging work environment. The company's commitment to its core values, such as "Deliver WOW Through Service" and "Create Fun and a Little Weirdness," has created a loyal customer base and a dedicated team of employees. Zappos' culture of empowerment and autonomy allows employees to make decisions that enhance customer experiences and drive business growth.

In the tech industry, companies like Netflix have also built strong corporate cultures that prioritize innovation and excellence. Netflix's culture is based on principles such as freedom and responsibility, which empower employees to take ownership of their work and make decisions that align with the company's goals. The company's commitment to hiring and retaining top talent is reflected in its practices of providing candid feedback, fostering a culture of continuous improvement, and rewarding high performance. This approach has enabled Netflix to stay ahead in the competitive streaming industry.

A strong corporate culture is not limited to tech companies. For instance, Johnson & Johnson's Credo, which outlines the company's responsibilities to customers, employees, communities, and shareholders, has guided its corporate culture for decades. The company's commitment to ethical business practices, social responsibility, and employee well-being has earned it a reputation as a trusted and respected leader in the healthcare industry.

In the next chapter, we will explore the importance of adaptability and resilience in the face of challenges and disruptions. Industry giants must navigate a constantly changing business landscape and demonstrate the ability to adapt and thrive in the face of adversity.

9

Chapter 9: Adaptability and Resilience: Navigating Challenges and Disruptions

In an ever-changing business landscape, the ability to adapt and demonstrate resilience in the face of challenges and disruptions is crucial for long-term success. Industry giants that can pivot, innovate, and navigate uncertainty are better positioned to thrive and maintain their competitive edge.

The COVID-19 pandemic is a prime example of how companies have had to adapt to unprecedented challenges. Businesses across various industries faced disruptions to their operations, supply chains, and customer interactions. However, companies that demonstrated agility and resilience were able to navigate the crisis effectively. For instance, many retailers quickly adapted to the surge in e-commerce demand by enhancing their online presence, implementing contactless delivery options, and optimizing their supply chains. Companies like Walmart and Target invested in their digital capabilities and omnichannel strategies, enabling them to meet customer needs and maintain business continuity.

In the tech industry, companies like Zoom experienced rapid growth as remote work and virtual communication became essential during the pandemic. Zoom's ability to scale its infrastructure, enhance security features, and provide reliable service allowed it to become a vital tool for businesses, educational institutions, and individuals worldwide. The company's adaptability and responsiveness to user feedback played a key role in its success during this period.

Similarly, in the automotive industry, companies like General Motors (GM) demonstrated resilience by pivoting their production capabilities to support pandemic response efforts. GM partnered with healthcare organizations to produce ventilators and personal protective equipment (PPE) to address critical shortages. This adaptability not only contributed to public health efforts but also showcased the company's commitment to social responsibility.

Industry giants also navigate challenges related to technological advancements and market disruptions. For example, the rise of digital streaming services has disrupted the traditional media and entertainment industry. Companies like Disney have adapted to this shift by launching their own streaming platforms, such as Disney+, to compete with established players like Netflix and Amazon Prime Video. Disney's strategic investments in content creation, technology, and global expansion have positioned it as a formidable competitor in the streaming market.

In the next chapter, we will explore the role of corporate social responsibility (CSR) in shaping the reputation and impact of industry giants. Companies that prioritize ethical practices, sustainability, and community engagement can create positive social and environmental outcomes while driving business success.

10

Chapter 10: Corporate Social Responsibility: Making a Positive Impact

Corporate social responsibility (CSR) is an integral aspect of modern business, shaping the reputation and impact of industry giants. Companies that prioritize ethical practices, sustainability, and community engagement create positive social and environmental outcomes while driving business success.

One notable example of CSR is Patagonia, an outdoor apparel company known for its commitment to environmental sustainability. Patagonia's mission statement, "We're in business to save our home planet," reflects its dedication to protecting the environment. The company implements sustainable practices throughout its supply chain, including using recycled materials, reducing carbon emissions, and promoting fair labor standards. Patagonia also donates a portion of its profits to environmental causes and encourages customers to repair and reuse their products through initiatives like Worn Wear. This commitment to CSR has earned Patagonia a loyal customer base and a reputation as a leader in environmental stewardship.

In the tech industry, companies like Microsoft have embraced CSR by focusing on sustainability, accessibility, and philanthropy. Microsoft's commitment to achieving carbon neutrality and investing in renewable energy demonstrates its dedication to environmental responsibility. The company also prioritizes accessibility, developing technologies that empower people with disabilities. Through the Microsoft Philanthropies initiative, the company supports various social causes, including education, digital inclusion, and disaster response. These efforts reflect Microsoft's commitment to making a positive impact on society.

Similarly, in the retail sector, companies like IKEA have integrated sustainability into their business model. IKEA's People & Planet Positive strategy aims to create a sustainable and circular business by focusing on resource efficiency, renewable energy, and sustainable sourcing. The company has committed to using only renewable and recycled materials in its products by 2030 and supports initiatives that promote sustainable living among its customers. IKEA's CSR efforts contribute to its brand reputation and align with the growing consumer demand for environmentally responsible products.

Corporate social responsibility also extends to social initiatives. Companies like Ben & Jerry's are known for their activism and advocacy on social issues, such as climate justice, racial equality, and LGBTQ+ rights. Ben & Jerry's uses its platform to raise awareness, engage in advocacy campaigns, and support grassroots organizations. The company's commitment to social justice is embedded in its values and business practices, resonating with consumers who prioritize ethical and socially responsible brands.

In the next chapter, we will explore the role of leadership in shaping the vision, culture, and success of industry giants. Effective leadership is essential for navigating challenges, driving innovation, and inspiring teams to achieve their full potential.

11

Chapter 11: Leadership: Guiding Vision and Inspiring Success

Effective leadership is a cornerstone of business success, shaping the vision, culture, and performance of industry giants. Strong leaders inspire their teams, navigate challenges, and drive innovation, creating a positive and dynamic work environment.

One iconic leader is Jeff Bezos, the founder of Amazon. Bezos' visionary leadership has transformed Amazon from an online bookstore into a global e-commerce and technology powerhouse. His customer-centric approach, long-term thinking, and willingness to take risks have driven Amazon's growth and innovation. Bezos' leadership principles, such as "Customer Obsession" and "Invent and Simplify," have become integral to Amazon's culture, guiding employees to prioritize customer needs and continuously innovate.

Another influential leader is Mary Barra, the CEO of General Motors (GM). Barra's leadership has been instrumental in steering GM through a period of significant transformation, including the shift towards electric vehicles and autonomous driving technology. Her focus on innovation, sustainability, and inclusion has positioned GM as a forward-thinking and resilient company. Barra's commitment to fostering a diverse and inclusive work environment has also contributed to GM's success and positive reputation.

In the tech industry, Satya Nadella, the CEO of Microsoft, has revitalized the company's culture and strategy since taking the helm in 2014. Nadella's emphasis on empathy, collaboration, and growth mindset has transformed Microsoft into a more agile and innovative organization. Under his leadership, Microsoft has embraced cloud computing, AI, and digital transformation, driving significant growth and market leadership. Nadella's inclusive leadership style and focus on corporate social responsibility have also strengthened Microsoft's reputation and impact.

Leadership is not limited to CEOs; it extends to leaders at all levels of an organization. Effective leaders empower their teams, promote a culture of continuous learning, and create an environment where employees feel valued and motivated. Companies like Google and Netflix prioritize leadership development, providing training and resources to help managers and leaders succeed in their roles.

In the next chapter, we will explore the future trends and opportunities that will shape the business landscape. Industry giants must stay ahead of emerging trends and leverage new technologies to maintain their competitive edge and drive sustained growth.

12

Chapter 12: The Future: Trends and Opportunities Shaping the Business Landscape

As we look to the future, several trends and opportunities will shape the business landscape and influence the strategies of industry giants. Companies must stay ahead of these trends to maintain their competitive edge and drive sustained growth.

One significant trend is the continued advancement of artificial intelligence (AI) and machine learning. These technologies have the potential to transform various industries by automating tasks, enhancing decision-making, and improving customer experiences. Industry giants like IBM, Google, and Amazon are investing heavily in AI research and development to unlock new capabilities and applications. AI-driven innovations, such as autonomous vehicles, personalized healthcare, and smart cities, will create new opportunities for businesses to innovate and grow.

Another emerging trend is the rise of the gig economy and remote work. The COVID-19 pandemic accelerated the adoption of remote work, and many companies have since embraced flexible work arrangements as a permanent fixture. Industry giants like Zoom and Slack have capitalized on this trend by providing tools and platforms that facilitate remote collaboration and communication. Companies must adapt to the changing workforce dynamics and develop strategies to attract and retain talent in a remote-first world.

Sustainability and environmental responsibility will continue to be critical drivers of business success. Consumers, investors, and regulators are increasingly demanding that companies adopt sustainable practices and reduce their environmental impact. Industry giants like Tesla, Unilever, and IKEA are leading the way in sustainability by implementing renewable energy solutions, circular economy models, and environmentally friendly products. Companies that prioritize sustainability will not only benefit from enhanced brand reputation but also contribute to a more sustainable future.

The digital transformation of industries will also create new opportunities for growth and innovation. Companies in sectors such as healthcare, finance, and retail are leveraging digital technologies to enhance their operations, improve customer experiences, and drive efficiency. For example, telemedicine platforms are transforming healthcare delivery by providing remote consultations and monitoring. In finance, blockchain technology is enabling secure and transparent transactions. Retailers are using augmented reality (AR) and virtual reality (VR) to create immersive shopping experiences. Industry giants must stay at the forefront of digital transformation to remain competitive and meet evolving consumer needs.

Finally, the importance of diversity, equity, and inclusion (DEI) in the workplace cannot be overstated. Companies that prioritize DEI are better positioned to attract top talent, foster innovation, and create a positive work environment. Industry giants like Microsoft, Google, and Salesforce are committed to advancing DEI by implementing inclusive hiring practices, providing diversity training, and promoting a culture of belonging. Companies that champion DEI will not only benefit from a diverse and innovative workforce but also contribute to a more equitable society.

Tech Savvy and Land Legacy: Business Tactics of Industry Giants

In an era where technology drives progress and strategic land investments secure stability, industry giants have mastered the art of blending these two powerful elements to achieve unparalleled success. "Tech Savvy and Land Legacy: Business Tactics of Industry Giants" unveils the winning strategies of leading companies that have harnessed the synergy of technological innovation and strategic real estate to dominate their markets.

Through twelve insightful chapters, this book explores the tactics employed by renowned companies like Amazon, Google, Tesla, and Microsoft. From embracing cutting-edge technologies to making astute land acquisitions, these industry leaders have set themselves apart by continuously adapting to an ever-evolving business landscape. Readers will discover how companies leverage data analytics, foster a culture of innovation, and form strategic alliances to drive growth and maintain a competitive edge.

Additionally, the book delves into the importance of corporate culture, social responsibility, and effective leadership in shaping the vision and success of these giants. It highlights the role of adaptability and resilience in navigating challenges and disruptions, providing valuable lessons for businesses of all sizes.

"Tech Savvy and Land Legacy: Business Tactics of Industry Giants" is an essential read for entrepreneurs, business professionals, and anyone seeking to understand the dynamics of modern business success. Packed with real-world examples and actionable insights, this book offers a comprehensive guide to building a thriving and sustainable business in today's complex and interconnected world.

www.ingramcontent.com/pod-product-compliance
Lightning Source LLC
LaVergne TN
LVHW020744090526
838202LV00057BA/6219